SPACE

SPACE

Wade Cooper

make
believe
ideas

Let's explore the wonders
of asteroids and stars,
the sun, the moon and planets –
from Jupiter to Mars!
The space station and the Milky Way
can both be found in space.
It is massive and incredible –
a truly amazing place!

Picture credits
(t-top, b-bottom, m-middle, l-left, r-right)
ESA/NASA/SOHO 10, 31br; NASA/HQ cover m, 3, 20-21, 29tr; NASA International Space Station Imagery
cover tl, 23mr, 32; NASA/John Hopkins University Applied Physics Laboratory/Carnegie Institution
of Washington 14t, 15l; NASA/JPL cover ml, 1, 14m, 17tr, 17mr, 26-27, 27b, 28mr, 28br, 29ml, 31ml;
NASA/JPLCaltech 9, 31tr; NASA/JPL-Caltech/Harvard-Smithsonian CfA cover bl, 30ml;
NASA/JPL/Caltech/Steve Golden 30tr; NASA/JPL-Caltech/University of Arizona 15br, 16b, 31mr;
NASA/JPL/Cornell University 5, 24-25; NASA/JPL/GSFC 28tl; NASA/JPL/Space Science Institute 16m;
NASA/JPL/STScI 17m; NASA/JPL/USGS 28bl, 31bl; NASA/JSC back cover, 3, 4, 18, 30br;
NASA/KSC 19; NASA/MSFC 22-23

Reading together

This book is an ideal early reader for your child, combining simple words and sentences with stunning colour photography. Here are some of the many ways you can help your child take those first steps in reading. Encourage your child to:

- Look at and explore the detail in the pictures.
- Sound out the letters in each word.
- Read and repeat each short sentence.

Look at the pictures

Make the most of each page by talking about the pictures and spotting key words. Here are some questions you can use to discuss each page as you go along:

- Why do you like this picture?
- What does it show?
- What do you think it would be like to be there?

Sound out the words

Encourage your child to sound out the letters in any words he or she does not know. Look at the common "key" words listed at the back of the book and see which of them your child can find on each page.

Test understanding

It is one thing to understand the meaning of individual words, but you need to check that your child understands the facts in the text.

- Play "spot the obvious mistake". Read the text as your child looks at the words with you, but make an obvious mistake to see if he or she has understood. Ask your child to correct you and provide the right word.
- After reading the facts, shut the book and make up questions to ask your child.
- Ask your child whether a fact is true or false.
- Provide your child with three answers to a question and ask him or her to pick the correct one.

Quiz pages

At the end of the book there is a simple quiz. Ask the questions and see if your child can remember the right answers from the text. If not, encourage him or her to look up the answers.

Space

What is in space?
People want to know.
Men and women
make machines
that take pictures
of things in space.

This is a picture of a galaxy.
There are many, many
of them in space.
This is a special galaxy.
It is called the Milky Way.
Many, many stars are
in the Milky Way.
Our sun is one
of them.

Did you know?

The Milky Way has
about 400 billion stars.
Our sun is one of them.

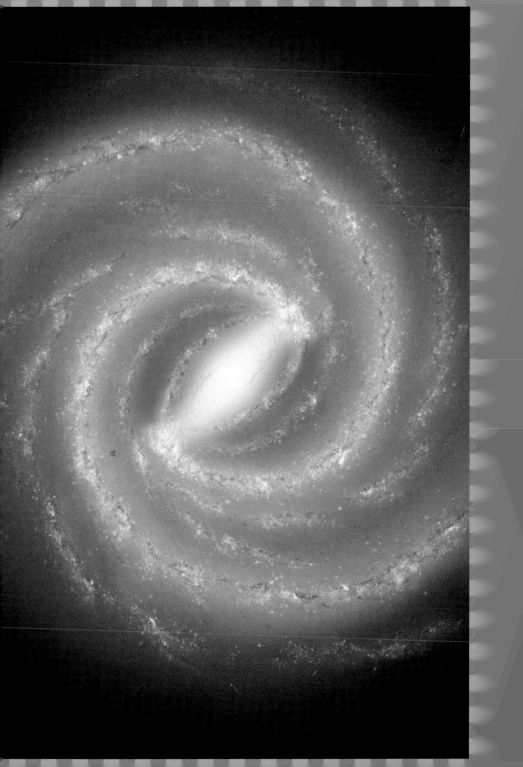

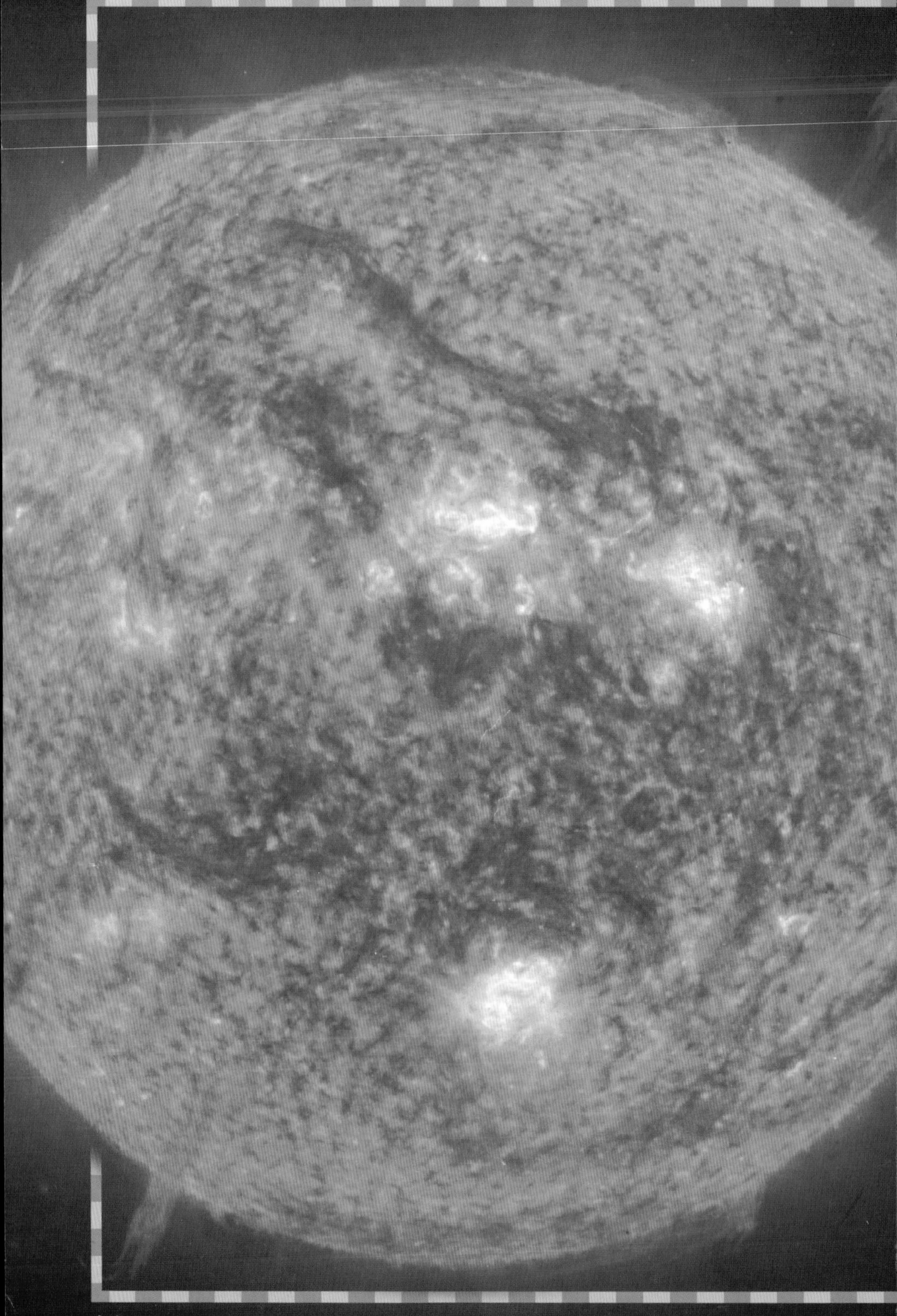

The sun is one star
in the Milky Way.
It is a ball
of burning gas.
It gives us heat
and energy
on Earth.

Did you know?

The sun is very large. You could fit
more than one million Earths inside it!

Neptune

Uranus

Saturn

Jupiter

M

Eight planets go
around the sun.
They are Mercury,
Venus, Earth, Mars,
Jupiter, Saturn,
Uranus and Neptune.

Did you know?

Asteroids go around the sun, too.
Asteroids are lumps of rock.

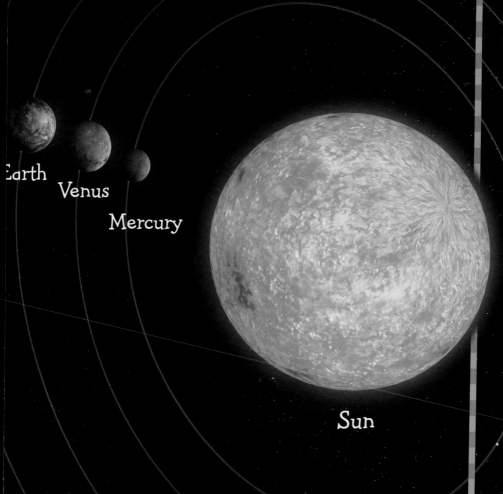

Earth

Venus

Mercury

Sun

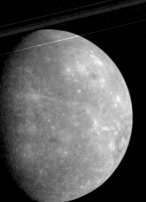

Mercury

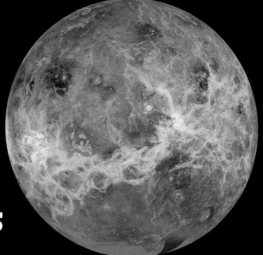

Venus

Did you know?

Earth takes 365 days to go around the sun one time.

Mercury, Venus,
Earth and Mars
are closest to the sun.
They are the hottest planets.
They are made of rock.

Earth

Mars

Jupiter, Saturn, Uranus
and Neptune are far
from the sun.
They are very cold.
They are made of gas
and liquid.
They are called
"gas giants".

Saturn

Jupiter

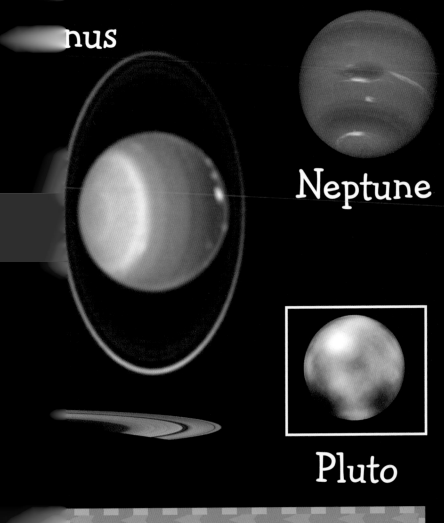

nus

Neptune

Pluto

Did you know?

People used to call Pluto a planet.
In 2006, people stopped calling
it a planet.

The first people to walk
on the moon were
Neil Armstrong and
Edwin "Buzz" Aldrin.
Michael Collins stayed
in the Command Module.

Did you know?

The little white cone holds the crew. It is the only part that will come back to Earth. It is called the Command Module.

Command Module

Armstrong and Aldrin
put an American flag
on the moon.

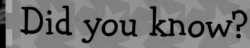

Did you know?

There is no air
on the moon.
Astronauts carry tanks
of air on their backs.

A space station is up in space. Scientists do experiments there.

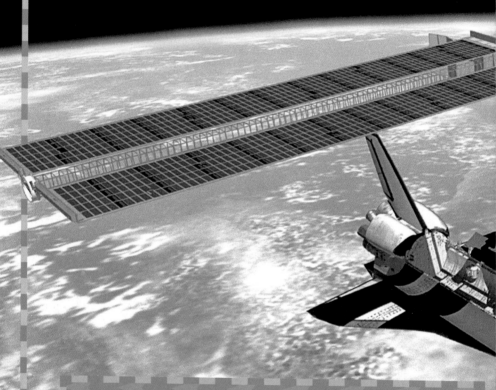

Did you know?

The space station goes around Earth almost 16 times a day.

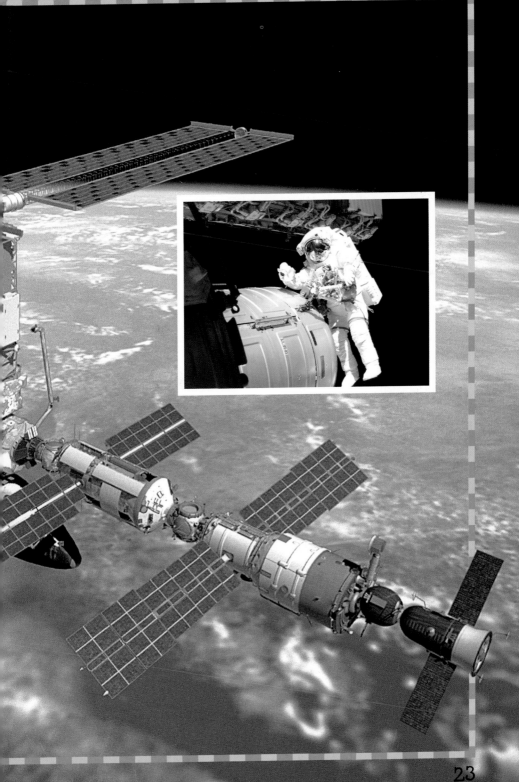

People have
many questions
about Mars.

Did you know?

Mars is rocky and
cold. There may be
water on Mars.

What does it look like?
Is there life on Mars?
People sent a robot to Mars.
The robot takes pictures
and sends them back
to Earth.

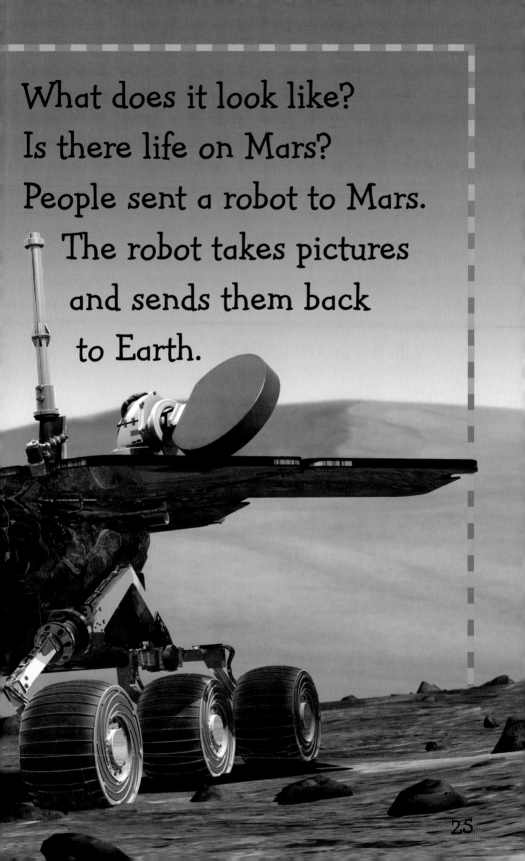

Deep Space 1 went
into space in 1998.
It sent back pictures
of a comet
and an asteroid.
Scientists stopped using
Deep Space 1
in December 2001.
But it is still
out in space.
It will not come back
to Earth.

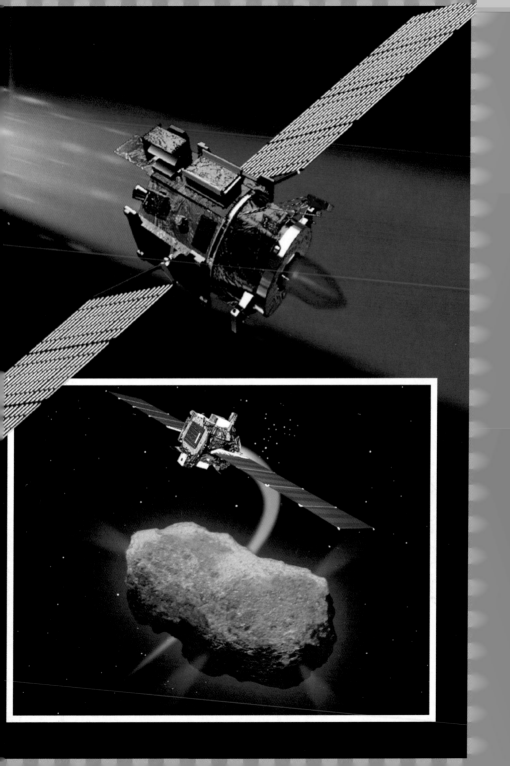

What do you know?

1. What is the Milky Way?

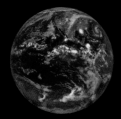

2. How many Earths would fit inside the sun?

3. How many planets go around the sun?

4. How long does it take Earth to orbit the sun?

5. Which four planets are closest to the sun?

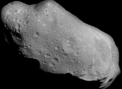

6. What is an asteroid?

7. Why are Saturn, Jupiter, Uranus and Neptune so cold?

8. Who were the first people to walk on the moon?

9. Why do astronauts need to carry air to breathe on the moon?

10. What is the sun?

11. What is Mars like?

12. What did *Deep Space 1* do?

Answers

1. The Milky Way is a galaxy. **2.** More than one million Earths would fit inside the sun. **3.** Eight planets go around the sun. **4.** Earth takes 365 days to orbit the sun. **5.** Mercury, Venus, Earth and Mars are the four planets closest to the sun. **6.** Asteroids are lumps of rock that orbit the sun. **7.** They are cold because they are so far from the sun. **8.** Neil Armstrong and Edwin "Buzz" Aldrin were the first people to walk on the moon. **9.** They need to carry air to breathe because there is no air on the moon. **10.** The sun is a ball of burning gas. **11.** It is rocky and cold. **12.** It sent back pictures of a comet and an asteroid.

Dictionary

stars
Stars are large and hot.
They make heat and light.

galaxy
A galaxy is a group
of stars.

planet
A planet travels
around the sun.

moon
A moon travels
around a planet.

astronaut
An astronaut is a person
who travels in space.

Key words

Here are some key words used in context.
Help your child to use other words from
the border in simple sentences.

There **are** many stars
in the Milky Way.

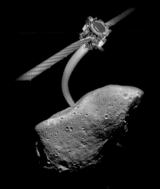

Deep Space 1 sent back
pictures **of** a comet.

Mars is rocky **and** cold.

There is **no**
air on the
moon.

The sun is **a** ball
of burning gas.

People of the past

Egypt is a hot country in north Africa. The people who lived there thousands of years ago are called ancient Egyptians.

This picture is part of an ancient Egyptian wall painting. It shows a group of servants.

Egyptian paintings often show things from the side.

River life

The ancient Egyptians built their towns and cities along a river called the Nile.

This photograph of Egypt was taken from space. The river and its banks look dark green.

Red Sea

River Nile —————

The yellow parts are dry, dusty deserts.

4

The Egyptians fished
in the river and
sailed boats on it.

They drank water
from it and used it
for washing clothes.

This is an ancient
Egyptian model
of a boat.

People swam in the Nile, but they
had to watch out for crocodiles.

Farmers

Egyptian farmers grew fruit, vegetables and other plants on the banks of the Nile.

This Egyptian painting shows farmers picking the grapes they have grown.

Farmers trained monkeys to pick fruit from high trees and throw it down.

The Nile flooded every year. This made the soil good for growing plants.

When the land dried up, plants grew in the sun. Farmers worked hard in the fields.

Farmers kept some of the crops to eat, and took the rest to markets.

At home

Ancient Egyptian houses were made of dried mud and painted white.

Houses had small windows to keep out the hot sun.

People cooked food and baked bread outside.

Some people had a pool in their garden where they kept fish to eat.

Egyptians slept on hard wooden beds,
with wooden headrests instead of pillows.

Rich people often had servants.
This model shows servants
hard at work baking bread.

Kings of Egypt

Egyptian kings were called pharaohs.
The pharaoh was the richest and most
important person in the whole country.

A pharaoh made
laws and gave orders.

He led his soldiers
to fight enemies.

He went out hunting
in his chariot.

He also met visitors
from other countries.

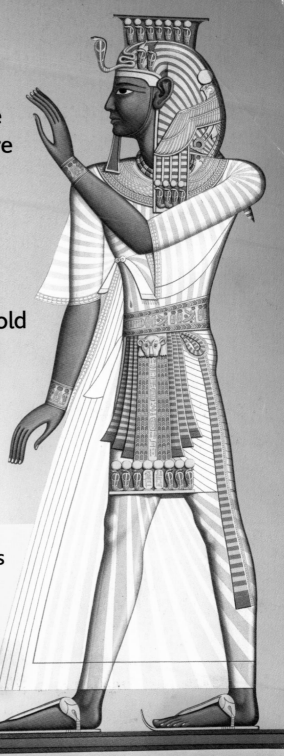

All pharaohs wore crowns. Some were decorated with gold and jewels.

This is a painting of Ramesses III. He is wearing a gold crown and a long, striped headdress.

Pharaoh Ramesses II had a pet lion to scare away enemies.

Gods and goddesses

Ancient Egyptians believed in many different gods and goddesses.

Egyptian gods sometimes looked like animals. This goddess, called Hathor, was often shown as a cow.

In this wall painting, Hathor has the horns of a cow on her crown.

12

Sekhmet was a fierce war goddess.

Ra was the powerful sun god.

Bes looked after children and families.

Ma'at was the goddess of truth.

Horus looked after pharaohs.

Seth was the evil uncle of Horus.

Horus and Seth were enemies. They once turned into fierce hippos to fight.

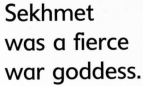

Temples

The Egyptians built huge stone temples to worship pharaohs and gods.

This is the temple of Pharaoh Ramesses II. Each statue outside the temple is more than ten times taller than a person.

14

In a temple, priests prayed to a statue of a god or pharaoh.

On special days, they carried the statue through the town.

This is a statue of Anubis, a god who could change into an animal called a jackal.

People often had small statues of gods at home, too.

Making a mummy

When an important person died, Egyptians wrapped their body so it didn't rot. This is called making a mummy.

1. First they took out the person's insides and put them in pots.

2. Then they packed the body in salt to dry it out.

3. Next, they wrapped the body tightly in bandages.

4. Finally, they put a mask on the mummy and laid it in a coffin.

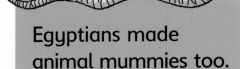

Egyptians made animal mummies too.

The person's insides were kept in pots with lids like these. Each pot has a god's head.

Coffins were shaped to look like a person and covered with spells and pictures.

Giant pyramids

When a pharaoh died, his coffin was put inside an enormous stone pyramid.

These large pyramids were built for three different pharaohs. The smaller pyramids were for their families.

Workers cut stone blocks and dragged them along.

They pulled the blocks up a ramp, onto the pyramid.

18

After many years of
work, they put the
last stone on top.

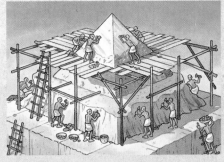

Finally, workers
made the pyramid
smooth and shiny.

Underground tombs

After many years, Egyptians stopped building pyramids. They buried important people in underground tombs instead.

1. First, workers dug a deep tunnel into a rocky cliff.

2. Then they built rooms and corridors underground.

3. They painted the walls and filled the rooms with treasure.

4. They put the coffin inside a huge box in a special room.

This is the tomb of a man named Peshedu.
His coffin lay in the room through this arch.

Robbers often dug into tombs
and pyramids to steal treasure.

Hidden treasure

The tomb of the pharaoh Tutankhamun was hidden for thousands of years.

In 1922, explorers found a secret door, hidden behind rocks.

Inside were rooms crammed with glittering treasure.

It took ten years to clear the tomb and list all the amazing treasures.

This falcon was one of the many beautiful statues in the tomb.

This big, heavy
mask covered
the face of
Tutankhamun's
mummy.

It is made
of gold and
thin strips
of glass.

Fun and games

Egyptians loved sports and games, as well as music, dancing and parties.

Some people learned to play instruments, like this harp.

Men liked to have boating contests on the River Nile.

The team that pushed the other boat over won the game.

24

This painting shows a man hunting with his family. He is standing on a boat and throwing a stick at birds.

At parties, people enjoyed watching dancers perform all kinds of difficult moves.

Dressing up

Egyptians liked to look good. They wore simple, flowing clothes and lots of jewels.

This wide, gold necklace is shaped like a bird. It was made for a pharaoh.

People often put perfumed fat on their heads. As it melted, it made them smell nice.

Men and women wore loose, light skirts and dresses that kept them cool.

They decorated the clothes with rings, bracelets, necklaces and other jewels.

Everyone wore make-up too. They put lots of dark paint around their eyes.

Most people shaved their heads to keep cool. Adults usually wore wigs.

27

Egyptian writing

Egyptian writing was made up of lots of pictures called hieroglyphs.

People called scribes could read and write hieroglyphs. The statue below shows a scribe.

A scribe's job was to write letters and keep records.

He also had to teach children to read and write.

These hieroglyphs were painted on a tomb.
They are spells to protect a dead person.

Most ordinary people didn't have
a clue what hieroglyphs meant.

Glossary of Egyptian words

Here are some of the words in this book you might not know. This page tells you what they mean.

 pharaoh - the title ancient Egyptians gave their king.

 temple - a place where Egyptians went to worship gods and dead pharaohs.

 priest - a person who worked in a temple. Priests prayed to statues.

 mummy - a body that has been dried out to make it last for many years.

 tomb - a place under the ground where a person was buried.

 scribe - a person whose job was to read and write.

 hieroglyph - a picture or symbol. Egyptians wrote using hieroglyphs.

Websites to visit

If you have a computer, you can find out more about the ancient Egyptians on the Internet. On the Usborne Quicklinks website there are links to four fun websites.

Website 1 - Play an Egyptian board game with a friend.

Website 2 - See your name in hieroglyphs.

Website 3 - Read about lots of different gods and goddesses.

Website 4 - Print out Egyptian pictures to crayon.

To visit these websites, go to **www.usborne-quicklinks.com** and type the keywords "beginners egyptians". Then click on the link for the website you want to visit. Before you use the Internet, look at the safety guidelines inside the back cover of this book and ask an adult to read them with you.

Index

Acknowledgements

Photographic manipulation by Emma Julings

Photo credits

The publishers are grateful to the following for permission to reproduce material:
© **Alamy** 18–19, 31 (Brian Lawrence); © **The Ancient Art and Architecture Collection Ltd** 12;
© **The Art Archive** 17b (Musée du Louvre Paris/Dagli Orti); © **Copyright The British Museum** 5, 17t, 24;
© **Corbis** 2–3, 6, 9, 21 (all Gianni Dagli Orti), 1, 15, 22 (all Sandro Vannini), 25 (Archivo Iconografico, S.A.),
26 (Bettman), 28 (Roger Wood), 29 (Wolfgang Kaehler); © **Digital Vision** back cover;
© **Getty Images** 14 (Richard Passmore), 23 (Alvis Upitis); © **Heritage Images**
11 (The British Library); © **NASA** 4 (Jacques Descloitres, MODIS Land Science Team)

Every effort has been made to trace and acknowledge ownership of copyright. If any rights have
been omitted, the publishers offer to rectify this in any subsequent editions following notification.